CREEPY, KOOKY SCIENCE

Deep-Sea Creatures

Roxanne Troup

Enslow Publishing
101 W. 23rd Street
Suite 240
New York, NY 10011
USA
enslow.com

Published in 2020 by Enslow Publishing, LLC
101 W. 23rd Street, Suite 240, New York, NY 10011

Library of Congress Cataloging-in-Publication Data

Names: Troup, Roxanne, author.
Title: Deep-sea creatures / Roxanne Troup.
Description: New York : Enslow Publishing, 2020. I Series: Creepy, kooky science I Includes bibliographical references and index. I Audience: Grade 5-8.
Identifiers: LCCN 2019005494I ISBN 9781978513723 (library bound) I ISBN 9781978513716 (paperback)
Subjects: LCSH: Deep-sea animals—Juvenile literature.
Classification: LCC QL125.5 .T76 2020 I DDC 597/.63—dc23
LC record available at https://lccn.loc.gov/2019005494

Printed in the United States of America

To Our Readers: We have done our best to make sure all websites in this book were active and appropriate when we went to press. However, the author and the publisher have no control over and assume no liability for the material available on those websites or on any websites they may link to. Any comments or suggestions can be sent by email to customerservice@enslow.com.

Contents

Introduction

What is it like to walk on the moon? How long does it take to travel one light-year? What is the weather like on Saturn? There is much to learn about space, but scientists currently know more about Mars than they know about the ocean! Marine scientists estimate that 95 percent of Earth's oceans is unexplored![1]

Modern oceanography didn't begin until 1872. That Christmas, six scientists set sail aboard a retired British warship named *Challenger*. Their job was to map the ocean floor, catalog marine life, and track the ocean's currents. For four years, these men sailed around the world collecting samples and measuring. They found the Mariana Trench, the deepest part of the ocean, and mapped part of the Mid-Atlantic Ridge. And they discovered more than 4,700 new species of plants and animals.[2]

The Challenger Expedition inspired others to study the ocean, too. In 1930, Otis Barton (1899–1992) and Dr. William Beebe (1877–1962) became the first to see deep-sea creatures in their natural habitat. Their vessel, the bathysphere, wasn't fancy.

It didn't even have an engine. It had to be lowered into the ocean's deep, dark cold by cables. There was just enough room in that steel ball for the explorers to sit side by side with their knees pulled up to their chins. Barton and Beebe's first dive took them 803 feet (245 m) into the deep.

Then, in 1934, they dove one-half mile (0.8 km) down. Dr. Beebe wrote about their experiences. He described the dark and the cold. He told of see-through fish. He tried to explain the strange flashing lights they witnessed.[3] Dr. Beebe wrote, "Most of the creatures at which I was looking were unnamed and had never been seen by any man."[4]

Dr. Beebe named four new fish on his dives into the deep. But many oceanographers didn't believe what he saw. Others thought he mistook known species for something new.[5] Because no one has seen Dr. Beebe's fish since, scientists still argue about it.[6] But with 1,500 new marine species identified each year, researchers may find the bathysphere fish yet.[7]

Between 1930 and 1934, Dr. William Beebe (*left*) and Otis Barton dove together more than thirty times in their 5,000-pound (2,268-kg) bathysphere.

In 1960, Jacques Piccard (1922–2008) and US Navy lieutenant Don Walsh (1931–) made it to the bottom of the ocean. Their ship, the *Trieste*, looked like a

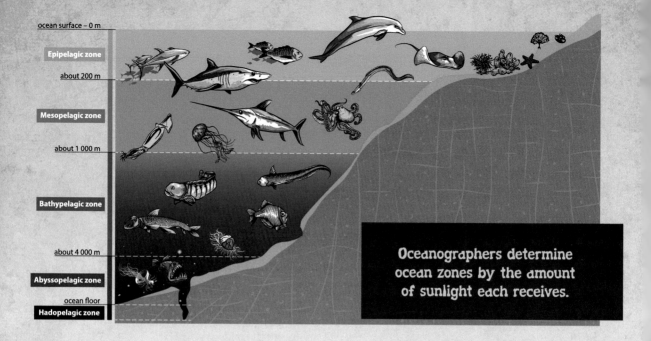

ocean surface – 0 m

Epipelagic zone

about 200 m

Mesopelagic zone

about 1 000 m

Bathypelagic zone

about 4 000 m

Abyssopelagic zone

ocean floor

Hadopelagic zone

Oceanographers determine ocean zones by the amount of sunlight each receives.

bathysphere with a long balloon on top. It dove 35,800 feet (10,912 m)—nearly 7 miles (11 km)—into the Mariana Trench. This deepest part of the ocean is called Challenger Deep. It is named after the famous Challenger Expedition that discovered the trench. Here the pressure of the water is so great, scientists didn't think life could exist. What Piccard and Lieutenant Walsh saw proved them wrong.[8]

Each dive into the depths reveals something new about the ocean and the creatures that live there. In order to make their jobs easier, oceanographers divide the ocean into zones. The zone closest to the surface is called the epipelagic or sunlit zone. This part of the ocean receives enough sunlight to grow plants. Most of the marine creatures people are familiar with live here: dolphins, seahorses, tuna, swordfish. But what lives below this zone? What did Barton and Beebe see in the deep, dark cold? What kind of life did Piccard and Walsh discover? Experts are still finding out!

CHAPTER 1

Barreleye Fish: Tiny Submarines

Just below the sunlit zone is the mesopelagic or twilight zone. *Mesopelagic* is a Greek word that means "middle sea." This zone extends from roughly 650 feet (198 m) below the surface of the water to a little more than 3,000 feet (914 m). It is cold and gets very little light from the sun.[1] Its deep midnight blue looks like the night sky. It even twinkles. Many of the creatures that live here are bioluminescent. They make their own light. Others have huge eyes to absorb as much light as possible in the near-dark ocean.[2]

The barreleye fish is a small fish that lives in the twilight zone. It has big barrel-shaped eyes covered by green lenses. The lenses filter sunlight so the barreleye can see the bioluminescent flashes of its prey.

This image taken in 2004 and provided by scientists at the Monterey Bay Aquarium Research Institute shows the barreleye's remarkable transparent head and bright green eyes.

The barreleye was discovered in 1939. But oceanographers couldn't figure out how this curious fish survived. The body of every 6-inch (15-cm) fish they caught was damaged in the nets on the way up to the surface. For more than fifty years, marine biologists wondered why its huge barrel eyes pointed straight up. How could it eat? How did it avoid predators and obstacles? It wasn't until 2004 that they realized part of the fish had been missing in all of the specimens they had seen![3]

Is That a Brain?

In 2004, the first live barreleye fish was found off the coast of California. Two researchers at the Monterey Bay Aquarium

Research Institute caught the first glimpse on a remotely operated vehicle (ROV) camera. Oceanographers use ROVs to study the ocean. These underwater robots are attached to a ship by cable. The cable allows the ROV and those onboard the ship to communicate with one another. Most ROVs are equipped with lights, cameras, and sampling devices. Some collect data about ocean temperature and water purity. Scientists operate ROVs like one would operate a remote-control car or video game. Researchers drive ROVs along the bottom of the ocean or propel them through the water. They can guide their sampling arms and tell them what samples to collect. Scientists use ROVs in places that are too dangerous for humans.[4]

The Monterey Bay Aquarium's video showed a submarine-shaped barreleye hovering in the water 2,000 feet (609 m) below the surface. Its eyes glowed green. And its head was transparent! Scientists had never seen that before. In every sample they had studied, that part of the head had been missing. The top section of a barreleye's head is filled with clear liquid. Its large eyes sit under this delicate shield. They look like they are wearing a pair of googly-eye glasses![5]

ROVs help oceanographers study life deep underwater without disturbing marine habitats.

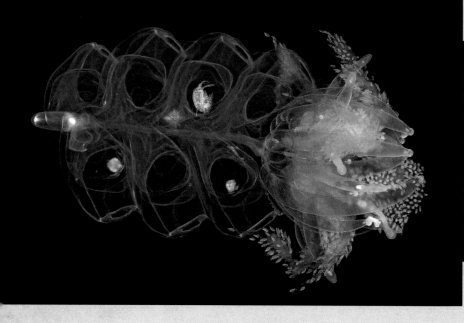

Scientists believe these "glasses" or lenses work like binoculars. The lenses allow the fish to zoom in on its prey. The barreleye can direct its eyes straight up or straight out. This way the fish can watch for potential prey above its clear head or rotate its eyes forward to focus on eating.

The two spots outside a barreleye's dome and above its tiny mouth aren't eyes. They are nares. Nares are fish nostrils. Unlike humans, fish do not use their nostrils to breathe. (That's what gills are for.) A fish's nares do not connect to its mouth, throat, and lungs like the human nose. Instead, nares open to sensory pads the fish use for detecting smells. These chemical smells alert fish to danger. They also help them find mates or prey.

A Fishy Thief

Barreleye fish also have large, flat fins. They wave and rotate these fins to keep themselves balanced. Barreleye can rest nearly motionless in the water as they wait for prey. Their fins also allow the fish to make the precise movements necessary to catch prey. When a tasty jellyfish is spotted above, the barreleye swims into position. Marine biologists at Monterey Bay Aquarium think barreleye may steal their food from jellyfish and siphonophores. They may also prey on jellies. Two of the fish the researchers studied had jellyfish fragments in their stomachs.

As the barreleye swims upward, it rotates its eyes to look straight ahead. It can now see its own mouth pointing toward the target. Using its fins, the barreleye swims in close to the tentacles of the jelly. Trapped in the stinging tentacles is a tiny shrimp. The fish grabs at the shrimp with its beaklike mouth. It darts away victorious.

But what happens if the barreleye misses its mark? Researchers from the Monterey Bay Aquarium think the fish's transparent dome acts as a shield. The dome protects the fish's eyes from the stinging tentacles of the jelly.[7]

Working Together

Siphonophores are cousins to the jellyfish. They usually grow in the shape of a rope and can be more than 33 feet (10 m) long! Siphonophores are colonial animals. Colonial animals are groups of animals that live and work together as one. They cannot survive alone. For example, some members of a siphonophore colony are in charge of swimming. Others are in charge of feeding. Still others are in charge of reproduction. The swimming members cannot feed themselves. The feeding members cannot swim. Each member of the colony must work together to survive.[6]

CHAPTER 2

Culper Eels: Nature's Balloon Animals

A t about 3,000 feet (914 m), the next oceanic zone begins. It is called the bathypelagic or midnight zone. *Bathypelagic* is a Greek word meaning "deep sea." No light penetrates this far into the ocean. The waters are still and quiet. It is near freezing.[1] The only warmth found this deep is near underwater chimneys called hydrothermal vents.

Hydrothermal vents form in volcanic areas. As seawater seeps through cracks on the seafloor, it heats up. The superheated water melts some of the metals in the rock before bursting back into the ocean like a geyser. The water cools. The chemicals solidify into rock. The water cycles. Layers and layers of rock build up. It forms a chimney. Water spews from the chimney in black or white plumes depending on its chemical makeup. It looks like the chimney is belching smoke. So scientists nicknamed them "smokers."[2]

This area of the ocean is difficult for oceanographers to explore. They send in ROVs for sampling and photographs. But ROV operators must be careful. If an ROV passes too close to a hydrothermal vent, the water could melt some of its parts!

Underwater hydrothermal vents are some of the hottest places on Earth. Black smokers heat water 3.5 times beyond its boiling point (212°F/100°C), but it doesn't boil! The water pressure is too extreme.

At Home in the Deep

Here, in the bathypelagic zone, a strange eel-like fish lives. This fish belongs to a family of deep-sea eels with huge mouths. It is called a gulper eel. The gulper has a hinged lower jaw and a pelican-like pouch in its throat. The jaw unhooks. The pouch inflates. Now this mysterious fish can gulp its prey whole.

Gulper eels go by many names. Pelican eel, whiptail gulper, and umbrella-mouth gulper are the most common. But gulper eels are not true eels. They are soft-bodied fish with long slender tails. Gulpers use their whip-like tails to move through the water. A tiny bioluminescent barb caps its tail.[3]

A gulper eel's hinged jaw allows it to swallow food whole. But new evidence shows that gulpers may also inflate their unusual mouths to appear larger and scare away predators.

Scientists don't know much about gulper eels. They are rare animals that live deep in the water. Finding one in the wild is unusual. When a team of seamount researchers off the coast of Hawaii saw a gulper swim into view on their ROV camera, it took a moment to realize what they were looking at. The purple-black creature sat floating in the water like a big round balloon. It had beady eyes and a long tail. Zooming in closer, they saw the creature shake its balloon body and open its huge jaw. One of the researchers finally recognized it as a gulper eel. Then before their eyes, it deflated back to normal size. It looked like a folded umbrella.[4]

Ambush Hunter?

Because scientists rarely see live gulper eels, they can only guess at how they live. They know gulper eels are dark to help them hide in the deep. They know gulper eyes and teeth are small. They know gulper tails are equipped with a glow-in-the-dark bulb. And they know

The Tallest Mountains

Seamounts are underwater mountains. They are typically formed by volcanic activity. Underwater, lava cools quickly into rock. As lava piles grow, they can break the ocean surface to form islands. One famous seamount is Mauna Kea. It is on the Big Island of Hawaii. This dormant volcano is the tallest mountain on Earth. Looking at Mauna Kea from sea level (the way all mountains are looked at), it appears small. But measured from its base on the seafloor to its peak, it is more than 32,000 feet (9,753 m)! That is nearly 3,000 feet (914 m) taller than Mount Everest.[5]

that both their throat pouches and stomaches can expand to more than twice their normal size. Experts just don't know why. Since researchers have only found pieces of squid, shrimp, and crustaceans in their stomachs, it doesn't seem likely that gulpers prey on larger species. So what is the purpose of the pelican-pouch?

Oceanographers use what they know to develop working theories about what they don't know. As they collect more data, they adjust those theories. One theory says the gulper eel hovers in the dark with its mouth open. It waits for food to fall into its mouth from above. Another theory says it waits with its tail curled toward its head. The bioluminescent end lures prey close—and gulp! Dinner.[6] Still another theory says the gulper uses its throat pouch like a net. When a troupe of shrimp swim past, the gulper scoops them up. It then sifts out the water through its gills and swallows the shrimp whole.[7] But new evidence may prove all these theories wrong.

In 2018, a team of researchers stumbled upon a gulper eel in the Atlantic. These scientists have been studying deep-sea creatures in the Azores region of Portugal for nearly thirty years. In a manned submersible 3,200 feet (975 m) below the surface, researchers caught the gulper in action. It seemed to be swimming after a fish! Researchers filmed the gulper for several minutes. They watched it expand its pouch and then swim toward the light of their submersible. The gulper snapped at something near the sub. The researchers think the gulper was hunting. If they are right, it may inspire a new working theory.[8]

CHAPTER 3

Anglerfish: Glow-in-the-Dark Fishermen

The most famous of the deep-sea creatures also lives in the bathypelagic zone. The anglerfish is a round fish that lures its prey with bioluminescence. Most anglers grow between 6 and 12 inches (15 to 30 cm) long. But some can grow as large as 3 feet (1 m). Their big mouths hang open and are full of sharp, jagged teeth.

Female anglerfish lure prey with bioluminescence, but they don't make their own light. Glowing bacteria live in their lures. The lure provides safety while the bacteria attract prey.

Their teeth fit together like the bars of a jail cell. Once inside, no prey can escape. The angler's unusual jaw and stretchy throat allow it to catch fish and shrimp twice its size!

Anglerfish are one of the deep sea's most fearsome predators. They will attack anything that comes near their mouths. In some parts of the world, anglerfish are called sea devils. With their strange appearance and sharp teeth, it's no wonder.[1]

Protecting the Oceans

Anglers are rarely encountered in the wild. But they are often caught in deep-sea trawlers. A trawler is a fishing boat that drags nets slowly through the water or along the ocean bottom to catch fish or shrimp. Trawlers allow fishermen to catch hundreds of fish at once. But these nets catch many other creatures as well. Fishermen throw unwanted creatures back into the ocean. But these creatures are often injured or killed in the nets. Nets can also destroy habitats. That is why many oceanographers want stricter trawling rules.[2]

No Beauty Contestant

Anglerfish are some of the most unusual-looking fish in the ocean. Their bodies are flabby. Their eyes are small. They have no scales. Anglerfish fins look like webbed toothpicks. Their heads are topped with a bony rod and lure that glows in the dark.

Food is scarce in the midnight zone. Predators there must adapt to survive. Their bodies must be equipped to handle the intense water pressure. They must be able to find food and spend energy wisely.

Anglers have adapted to life in the deep by becoming ambush predators. Their flabby bodies allow them to float and tumble through the water without much effort. Instead of swimming after prey, anglerfish wait in the dark for food to find them. The angler's head rod sticks out like a fishing pole. The bioluminescent lure becomes the bait. When a fish swims near to investigate the light, the angler strikes.[3]

There are more than 150 different species of deep-sea angler-fish.[4] They spend most of their lives at depths greater than 3,000 feet (914 m). Some anglerfish have even been found at depths of nearly one mile (1.6 km). The fanfin angler grows whisker-like filaments. Scientists think these whiskers act like antennae. They help the fish sense what is happening nearby as it floats in the water.[5] The whipnose anglerfish has a whip-like rod and lure that can be four times longer than its body.[6] Scientists recently found this fish swimming upside down! It seemed to be using its rod and lure to trawl along the seabed.[7]

Each species of anglerfish has adapted to survive in its specific environment. The coffinfish is a species of angler that looks like a toad. It doesn't swim but uses its fins to "stand" on the seafloor and wait for prey. When startled, the coffin-fish quickly pushes water through its gills. The rushing water pushes the fish out of harm's way. This jet propulsion is similar to the way a squid or jellyfish moves.[8]

Parasitic Mate

Anglerfish have also adapted in the way they mate. In most anglerfish species, the male angler is much smaller than the female. His body is more streamlined, which makes it easier to swim. But he doesn't have a large mouth. He doesn't have a lure. Without help he will die.

Two males have attached themselves to this female. The tiny male anglerfish has large eyes and humungous nares. He uses these senses to help find a mate in the dark depths of the ocean.

A male anglerfish spends his entire life looking for a female. He searches the midnight zone following the chemical scent female anglers produce. When he finds one, the male bites the female and hangs on! He releases an enzyme around the bite that dissolves the female's skin. It dissolves his teeth and mouth, too. Their bodies fuse. Their bloodstreams join. Now the male can live off the nutrients and oxygen in the female's blood. He doesn't need to hunt prey.

Several males may latch onto the same female. As the male angler fuses with the female, he loses his eyesight. His fins dissolve. All his organs shut down. He looks like a skin sack. The only part of the male anglerfish that continues to function is his reproductive organs. With both a female and male represented, the anglerfish can now spawn at will. When the female releases her eggs, the male fertilizes them in the water. Fertilized eggs float to the surface. They hatch under a mat of floating seaweed.[9] As they grow, the young anglerfish make their way back to the deep. The females develop lures and begin hunting. The males begin looking for mates, and the life cycle continues.

CHAPTER 4

Yeti Crabs: Furry Farmers

In March 2005, a team of oceanographers set out to explore hydrothermal vents near Easter Island in the Pacific Ocean. They launched a manned ROV named *Alvin* to help. During one of *Alvin*'s dives, a marine biologist saw an unusual creature. He asked the pilots to collect a sample. They brought it to the surface. It was a crab with hairy arms!

The *Alvin* team saw many such crabs living along the ocean floor. Most were near hydrothermal seeps or recent lava flows. A hydrothermal seep is similar to a hydrothermal vent. Instead of hot water spewing out of underwater chimneys, it seeps out of cracks on the seafloor.

The hairy crab reminded the *Alvin* team of an abominable snowman. So they started calling it a "yeti crab."[1] Its real name is *Kiwa hirsuta*. Kiwa is the Polynesian protector of the sea. *Hirsuta* is a Latin word that means "hairy."[2]

The spiky hairs of the yeti crab are called setae. Crabs use their setae to catch the bacteria that live in the waters near hydrothermal vents.

A Mother's Love

Crabs are cold-blooded. Cold-blooded animals depend on their environment to regulate body temperature. They can't do it themselves. Vent sites warm the deep ocean, so yeti crabs can live there. But livable space is small. Too close and the crabs will cook. Too far and they'll freeze. But crabs can't lay their eggs in this warm place. The eggs will be trampled. The babies won't develop. Mother crabs must leave the safety of the vent to lay their eggs. Most are too weak after brooding to travel back to the vent. But they have given their young a chance.[5]

Deep-Sea Farmers

Only a handful of Kiwa species have been found. They live scattered around the southern ocean. In some communities, yeti crabs have hairy chests instead of hairy arms. These fuzzy creatures are nicknamed "Hoff crabs." (They were nicknamed after American actor David Hasselhoff, who is well known for his hairy chest, which was often bared on the TV show *Baywatch*.) They heap up near hydrothermal vents in the cold waters of the Antarctic. In these vent communities, seventy crabs live in one square foot of space (that's seven hundred crabs per square meter)![3] No matter where yetis live—or where their hair grows—these crabs depend on chemosynthesis to survive. Chemosynthesis is the process of using chemicals instead of light to produce food.[4]

Yeti crabs are blind. They cannot scavenge for food. They grow their own! Hydrothermal vents are the perfect environment for bacteria. It is warm. And the bacteria use chemicals from the vents to make food. Yetis use their hairy bodies to collect and grow bacteria. Then they wave their arms in the chemical-rich waters. Scientists believe this feeds the bacteria like a farmer fertilizes his crops. Now the yeti has a constant supply of food!

Next-Door Neighbors

Yeti crabs live at depths of 6,500 to 8,500 feet (2,000 to 2,800 m). This far below the surface, water temperatures hover around freezing. Water from hydrothermal vents warms the area. It creates a pocket where life can thrive. Water from the vents can be 750 degrees Fahrenheit (400 degrees Celsius). But it cools quickly. Temperatures return to 35°F (1.6°C) within 3 feet (1 m) of a vent.[6] That doesn't leave much space for life. Yet hydrothermal vents are some of the most densely populated areas in the deep ocean.

Tubeworms taller than a man make their home at vent sites. These creatures have no spine. They have no eyes or mouth. And they grow up to 3 feet (1 m) per year! Tubeworms look like huge lipsticks. They survive in a symbiotic relationship with bacteria. Bacteria enter through the tubeworm's skin. Safe inside, they turn chemicals in the water into sugars the tubeworms can use for food.[7]

Oceanographers have also found vent clams the size of dinner plates and tiny shrimp without eyes in these communities. No humans will eat these common seafood products though. The chemicals in the water make them smell and taste like rotten eggs![8]

Giant tubeworms colonize a hydrothermal vent near the Galapagos Islands in the Pacific Ocean. To find new sites, tubeworms send their babies scouting. They drift in the water looking for the warmth of a vent. Then they swim down, attach to the new vent, and start growing.

The dumbo octopus also lives nearby. It is a small creature with two fins near the top of its mantle, a large muscle behind its head where all its organs are located. The fins look like ears. Dumbo octopuses flap and wave their fins to hover above the ocean floor. When a tasty snail or worm comes near, the octopus drops onto it. The octopus eats the snail whole. Dumbo octopuses belong to the umbrella octopus family. Their arms are connected with a skirt-like piece of skin. They look like open umbrellas when floating. The dumbo octopus is the deepest-living octopus known to science.[9]

CHAPTER 5

Giant Squid: Fact or Fiction?

The ocean has fascinated people and inspired stories for centuries. Ancient peoples believed the ocean was filled with monsters. They told stories about them. They decorated their maps with drawings of fantastic beasts. But where did these ideas come from? Could creatures from the abyssopelagic zone be the source of sea myths and man-eating monsters?

Abyssopelagic means "bottomless sea." This zone stretches 13,000 to 20,000 feet (4,000 to 6,000 m) deep. Here the ocean floor looks like a wrinkled bedsheet. But those "wrinkles" are really short, sharp ridges. For thousands of years, no one knew what creatures made their home in the "abyss." All they had were stories, and the occasional carcass that washed ashore.

The kraken legend was so well known in Norway, some thought it was science. In 1735, zoologist Carolus Linnaeus included the kraken, featured here in medieval artwork, in his classification of living animals.

One such story in Norway was written down nearly one thousand years ago. It told of a huge, multi-armed monster that sunk ships. They called it the kraken. Sailors repeated the kraken story everywhere they went. They added their own strange sightings to the tale. And soon the story was legend. It wasn't until the mid-1800s that the kraken was linked to a real creature. In 1873, Reverend Moses Harvey (1820–1901) bought a strange creature from an old fisherman. It was so big he had to drape it over his bathtub. He took its picture. It was a 27-foot (8-meter) giant squid![1]

Where the Giants Live

Water pressure in the abyss is two hundred to six hundred times that of the surface. If a Styrofoam cup fell into the abyss, its atoms would compress. The pressure would squeeze out all the air. The cup would look like a tiny thimble. This intense pressure is why most creatures of the abyssal zone are tiny. There is no air or "empty space" in their bodies.

But some creatures of the abyss are huge! Scientists think these creatures grow larger in response to the extreme pressure. Others think that creatures in the abyss never stop growing. The longer they live, the bigger they get. Creatures such as the giant isopod can grow to more than 1 foot (30 cm) long. Their on-land cousins, the pill bug, are less than 0.5 inch (1 cm) long.[2]

The giant squid is another unusually large creature of the deep. It has no bones. Like the octopus, the squid gets its shape from its mantle. The mantle also allows the squid to move quickly. At the base of the mantle is a small tube-like opening. It is called a siphon. To move, a squid sucks water into its mantle then pushes it out again through the siphon. The force of the water pushes the squid forward. Squid can rotate their siphon to change direction.[3]

A scientist measures a giant squid at Auckland University in New Zealand in 2013. While living, squid change color to match their surroundings and communicate with other creatures.

Squid arms are covered in rows of suckers. Each sucker is ringed with saw-like teeth that help it grab onto prey. Counting their arms, giant squid can grow to 43 feet (13 m). They have the largest eyes on the planet. Their eyes are the size of soccer balls. Scientists think these huge eyes allow giant squid to see bioluminescent flashes 393 feet (120 m) away.[4] If a predator comes near, the squid uses its siphon to get away. If the flashing lights are prey, the squid folds up its feeding tentacles then shoots them out like a rubber band.

Fierce Fighters

Giant squid eat fish and other squid. Their feeding tentacles can stretch 33 feet (10 m). This allows them to sneak up on prey. When a school of fish passes overhead, the squid jets up. It stretches out its tentacles and grabs a fish. The squid retreats to the safety of the deep.

Arms or Tentacles?

Squid and octopuses are cephalopods. *Cephalopod* is Latin for "head-foot." All ceph-alopods have limbs attached to their heads. These limbs are called arms. Cephalopod arms are covered in rows of suckers. Many mistakenly call them tentacles. A tentacle is not the same as an arm. Tentacles are long organs used for feeding and sensing danger. They have suction cups only on their tips. Some cephalopods let their ten-tacles dangle. Others keep them folded tight to the body. When needed, they stretch out to snatch prey. Octopuses have eight arms, no tentacles. Squid have eight arms and two tentacles.[5]

Its tentacle suckers hold the fish tight. In a safe place, it stops. The squid folds its tentacles closer to its body. Its arms grab the fish and push it toward the mouth. The squid's sharp beak tears the fish in pieces. Its tongue grinds the fish like sandpaper. A giant squid's tongue is covered in tiny teeth. They break and smash food pieces into a pulp the squid can swallow.[6]

Giant squid are toward the top of the food chain. But they still have predators. Sperm whales dive deep into the ocean to find food. They especially like squid. Giant squid beaks are often found in their stomachs. But giant squid don't go quietly. They are fierce fighters. Sperm whales bear the scars to prove it! Many accounts of sperm whales covered in round scars are reported each year. The bumpy scars are a perfect match to squid suckers. Some are so large they could only be made by the giant squid. Maybe the squid was trying to protect itself. Maybe it was trying to hold the whale underwater until the whale drowned. Maybe it needed a solid hold to bite the whale with its beak. Experts don't know. But they have yet to find a giant squid with pieces of whale in its belly![7]

CHAPTER 6

Sea Lilies and Sea Cucumbers: Not the Garden Variety

Deeper still is the hadopelagic zone. *Hadopelagic* comes from the Greek word for Hades. In Greek mythology, Hades was the god of the underworld. His home lay deep in the earth. It was also called Hades. The hadal zone of the ocean stretches into Earth's crust through trenches. It reaches "under" the world and includes habitats 20,000 to 36,000 feet (6,000 to 11,000 m) below the surface.[1]

Ocean trenches form where two tectonic plates meet. A tectonic plate is a large, slow-moving section of Earth's crust. When tectonic plates rub together, they cause earthquakes. When they push against each other, they can create mountains. But when tectonic plates overlap, they can create trenches and volcanoes.[2]

Ocean trenches in the hadal zone are covered in deep-sea mud. This mud is made up of decaying animals and crushed rock. All kinds of creatures live in it. Some are too tiny to see. Others are the size of a child's little finger. Most of these creatures eat seafloor mud. Their bodies filter nutrients out of the mud and eliminate the rest.[3] Some of the creatures in the hadal zone look like vegetables and flowers. But they are not backyard garden plants; they are animals.

Sea Lilies

Sea lilies are some of the largest creatures in the hadal zone. They are related to sea urchins and starfish. Their bodies are arranged in a circle. Their mouths are at the center. Arms extend out from their mouths like petals on a flower. A sea lily waves its arms in the water to catch microbes and tiny bits of food. The food is trapped in the lily's feathery arms and pushed toward its mouth.[4]

There are eighty different species of sea lilies currently living. They grow to lengths of 24 inches (60 cm). Scientists have identified five thousand extinct species of sea lilies. Some of them grew

Like starfish, sea lily arms grow in multiples of five.
Unlike their starfish cousins, sea lilies do not have
stomachs. They absorb nutrients in their intestines.

to 65 feet (20 m) long! Sea lilies make their homes in both shallow
and deep waters. They attach themselves to rocks or along the
ocean floor with a stalk. The stalk acts like an anchor. It keeps
them from drifting away like their cousins, the feather star. For
many years, scientists thought a sea lily's stalk kept the lily in one
place its entire life. But recent evidence suggests that sea lilies
can walk!

Deep-Sea Filters

Sea cucumbers act like deep-sea filters. They pick up ocean waste. As they eat, sand and mud pass through their digestive system. The sea cucumber absorbs organic material from the mud and recycles the rest. Anything the cucumber can't use is pushed out its anus. This clean poop helps keep the ocean healthy. Scientists think it may keep algae in check. In shallow waters, sea cucumber droppings feed plants on the coral reefs. Sea cucumbers are the ocean's version of an earthworm![6]

When a sea lily needs to move, it breaks off the end of its stalk like lizards break their tails. The sea lily then uses its feathery arms to creep across the seafloor. When it finds a suitable place to live, it anchors its stalk back to a rock or onto the seafloor.[5]

Sea Cucumbers

Sea cucumbers are some of the most numerous creatures in the hadal zone. A sea cucumber is a mud eater. It looks like a garden cucumber or slug. Some have leathery skin. Others are bumpy and spiky like the seafloor. All sea cucumbers move about on tiny tube-like feet. They are herding animals. They often travel in groups crawling along the seafloor searching for bits of food.

Sea cucumbers don't have a noticeable head. They have no eyes, and their mouths are on the seafloor side of their body. A sea cucumber's mouth works like a vacuum. It is circled by tiny tentacles. As the cucumber stirs up mud on the seafloor, the tentacles catch bits of broken sea lily stalk or shrimp leg. They push those bits into the sea cucumber's mouth.[7]

Sea cucumbers have some odd habits. They breathe through their anus. And when a sea cucumber is threatened, it shoots out its organs! The flying organs scare predators away. In some species, they are also toxic. If the sea cucumber manages to escape, it will regrow its organs in a couple of weeks.

Sea cucumbers live on the seafloor in both deep and shallow water. They belong to the same animal group, called echinoderms, as starfish and sea lilies.

Sea cucumbers and other deep-sea creatures are fascinating animals. But they are just a sampling of life in the deep. What else is out there to discover? How do these creatures contribute to the health of the ocean? Can these amazing creatures uncover the secrets of humanity's past? What role will they play in humanity's future? Only time—and science—will tell.

Chapter Notes

Introduction

1. Heidi Sosik, "The Discoveries Awaiting Us in the Ocean's Twilight Zone," Ted Talks, April 2018, https://www.ted.com/talks/heidi_m_sosik_what_if_we_explored_the_ocean_s_twilight_zone.

2. Woods Hole Oceanographic Institution, "The Challenger Expedition," Dive and Discover: Expeditions to the Seafloor, 2019, https://divediscover.whoi.edu/history-of-oceanography/the-challenger-expedition/.

3. William Beebe, *Half Mile Down* (New York, NY: Harcourt, Brace and Company, 1934), pp. 99–137, 157–175, https://www.biodiversitylibrary.org/item/40714#page/245/mode/1up.

4. Beebe, p. 165

5. "Steel Diving Bell Opens Door to New, Fantastic Undersea World," *Roanoke Rapids Herald*, September 13, 1934, https://chroniclingamerica.loc.gov/lccn/2017236974/1934-09-13/ed-1/seq-4/.

6. "History of the Study of Marine Biology," MarineBio Conservation Society, 2019, http://marinebio.org/oceans/history-of-marine-biology/.

7. "Discovering Unknown Species," *Science Illustrated*, September 1, 2018, https://www.pressreader.com/australia/science-illustrated/20180901/281595241346507.

8. "First Trip to the Deepest Part of the Ocean," Geology.com, 2019, https://geology.com/records/bathyscaphe-trieste.shtml.

Chapter 1. Barreleye Fish: Tiny Submarines

1. National Oceanic and Atmospheric Administration (NOAA), "Ocean Zones," Ocean Explorer, https://oceanexplorer.noaa.gov/edu/curriculum/section5.pdf (accessed January 30, 2019).
2. Rebecca Johnson, *Journey into the Deep: Discovering New Ocean Creatures* (Minneapolis, MN: Millbrook Press, 2011), pp. 18–19.
3. Richard A. Lovett, "First Photos: Weird Fish with Transparent Head," *National Geographic*, February 22, 2009, https://www.nationalgeographic.com/animals/2009/02/photo-transparent-fish-animals/.
4. Dr. Paul Yancey, "The Deep Sea," MarineBio Conservation Society, updated December 29, 2011, http://marinebio.org/oceans/deep/.
5. "Researchers Solve Mystery of Deep-Sea Fish with Tubular Eyes and Transparent Head," Monterey Bay Aquarium Research Institute, February 23, 2009, https://www.mbari.org/barreleye-fish-with-tubular-eyes-and-transparent-head/.
6. "Giant Siphonophore," Monterey Bay Aquarium, https://www.montereybayaquarium.org/animal-guide/invertebrates/giant-siphonophore (accessed January 9, 2019).
7. "Researchers Solve Mystery."

Chapter 2. Gulper Eels: Nature's Balloon Animals

1. Dr. Paul Yancey, "The Deep Sea," MarineBio Conservation Society, updated December 29, 2011, http://marinebio.org/oceans/deep.
2. Maya Wei-Hass, "Scientists Explore Breathtaking Hydrothermal Vents in Virtual Reality," *Smithsonian Magazine*, May 31, 2016, https://www.smithsonianmag.com/innovation/scientists-explore-breakthaking-hydrothermal-vents-virtual-reality-180959266/.
3. "Whiptail Gulper," Oceana.com, https://oceana.org/marine-life/ocean-fishes/whiptail-gulper (accessed Jan. 14, 2019).

4. "Gulper Eel Balloons Its Massive Jaws," *Nautilus* Live, September 20, 2018, https://nautiluslive.org/video/2018/09/20/gulper-eel-balloons-its-massive-jaws.

5. "Highest Mountain in the World," Geology.com, 2019, https://geology.com/records/highest-mountain-in-the-world.shtml.

6. "Creatures of the Deep Sea: Gulper Eel," Sea and Sky, 2016, http://www.seasky.org/deep-sea/gulper-eel.html.

7. Lori Cuthbert, "Watch a Gulper Eel Inflate and Deflate Itself, Shocking Scientists," *National Geographic*, September 21, 2018, https://www.nationalgeographic.com/animals/2018/09/gulper-eel-video-deep-sea-fish-nautilus-news/.

8. Frankie Schembri, "First Direct Observation of Hunting Pelican Eel Reveals a Bizarre Fish with an Inflatable Head," *Science Magazine*, October 4, 2018, https://www.sciencemag.org/news/2018/10/first-direct-observation-hunting-pelican-eel-reveals-bizarre-fish-inflatable-head.

Chapter 3. Anglerfish: Glow-in-the-Dark Fishermen

1. "Anglerfish," *National Geographic*, 2019, https://www.nationalgeographic.com/animals/fish/group/anglerfish/.

2. "Destructive Fishing," Marine Conservation Institute, https://marine-conservation.org/what-we-do/program-areas/how-we-fish/destructive-fishing/ (accessed January 21, 2019).

3. Erich Hoyt, *Creatures of the Deep: In Search of the Sea's Monsters and the World They Live In* (Buffalo, NY: Firefly Books, 2014), pp. 47–49, 58–59.

4. Elaina Zachos, "First-Ever Footage of Deep-Sea Anglerfish Mated Pair," *National Geographic*, March 23, 2018, https://news.nationalgeographic.com/2018/03/anglerfish-mating-rare-video-spd/.

5. Jacinta Bowler, "This Incredibly Rare Deep-Sea Video of Mating Anglerfish Is Stunning Biologists," Science Alert, March 23, 2018, https://www.sciencealert.com/this-beautiful-video-of-mating-deep-sea-anglerfish-is-stunning-biologists.

6. Dante Fenolio, *Life in the Dark: Illuminating Biodiversity in the Shadowy Haunts of Planet Earth* (Baltimore, MD: Johns Hopkins University Press, 2016), pp. 48, 96–99.

7. "So Many Mysteries of the Deep," Monterey Bay Aquarium Research Institute, September 30, 2012, https://www.mbari.org/bioluminescence-and-biodiversity-2013-sep-30/.

8. Bruce Mundy, "The Mysterious Identity of the Bright-Red Sea Toad," NOAA Fisheries, September 12, 2017, https://www.fisheries.noaa.gov/science-blog/mysterious-identity-bright-red-sea-toad.

9. Auckland War Memorial Museum, "Auckland Museum Expedition Finds Deep-Sea Angler Fish in Three Kings Island Seaweed," YouTube, April 11, 2013, https://www.youtube.com/watch?v=DvJEuBRNzfU.

Chapter 4. Yeti Crabs: Furry Farmers

1. "Discovery of the 'Yeti Crab,'" Monterey Bay Aquarium Research Institute, March 2006, https://www.mbari.org/discovery-of-yeti-crab.

2. Jasmin Fox-Skelly, "In the Deep Sea There Live 'Crabs' That Look Like Yetis," BBC Earth, April 13, 2017, http://www.bbc.com/earth/story/20170412-in-the-deep-sea-there-live-crabs-that-look-like-yetis.

3. Jason Bittel, "New Species: Hairy Chested Yeti Crab Found in Antarctica," *National Geographic*, June 24, 2015, https://news.nationalgeographiccom/2015/06/150624-new-species-yeti-crab-antarctica-oceans.

4. Rebecca Johnson, *Journey into the Deep: Discovering New Ocean Creatures* (Minneapolis, MN: Millbrook Press, 2011), p. 24.

5. Ali Berman, "Newly Discovered Yeti Crabs Pile on to Survive," Mother Nature Network, June 25, 2015, https://www.mnn.com/earth-matters/animals/stories/newly-discovered-yeti-crabs-pile-survive.

6. "Ocean Vent," *National Geographic*, 2019, https://www.nationalgeographic.org/encyclopedia/ocean-vent.

7. Kristen M. Kusek, "Deep-Sea Tubeworms Get Versatile 'Inside' Help," *OceanUs Magazine*, January 12, 2007, https://www.whoi.edu/oceanus/feature/deep-sea-tubeworms-get-versatile-inside-help.

8. Johnson, pp. 25, 50.

9. "Dumbo Octopus," Aquarium of the Pacific, 2019, https://www.aquariumofpacific.org/onlinelearningcenter/species/dumbo_octopus.

Chapter 5. Giant Squid: Fact or Fiction?

1. Grace Costantino and Biodiversity Heritage Library, "Five 'Real' Sea Monsters Brought to Life by Early Naturalists," *Smithsonian Magazine*, October 27, 2014, https://www.smithsonianmag.com/science-nature/five-real-sea-monsters-brought-life-early-naturalists-180953155/.

2. Dante Fenolio, *Life in the Dark: Illuminating Biodiversity in the Shadowy Haunts of Planet Earth* (Baltimore, MD: Johns Hopkins University Press, 2016), p. 64.

3. Dr. Clyde Roper, "Giant Squid," Smithsonian Education, April 2018, https://ocean.si.edu/ocean-life/invertebrates/giant-squid.

4. Ed Young, "Giant Squids Have Huge Eyes to See Shiny Charging Whales," *National Geographic*, January 27, 2013, https://www.nationalgeographic.com/science/phenomena/2013/01/27/giant-squids-have-huge-eyes-to-see-shiny-charging-whales.

5. "Cephalopods: Arms or Tentacles?" National Aquarium, October 3, 2017, https://www.aqua.org/blog/2017/October/Cephalopods-Arms-or-Tentacles.

6. Roper.

7. Erich Hoyt, *Creatures of the Deep: In Search of the Sea's Monsters and the World They Live In* (Buffalo, NY: Firefly Books, 2014), pp. 146–147.

Chapter 6. Sea Lilies and Sea Cucumbers: Not the Garden Variety

1. Dr. Paul Yancey, "The Deep Sea," MarineBio Conservation Society, updated December 29, 2011, http://marinebio.org/oceans/deep.

2. "Plate Tectonics," *National Geographic*, 2019, https://www.nationalgeographic.com/science/earth/the-dynamic-earth/plate-tectonics.

3. Erich Hoyt, *Creatures of the Deep: In Search of the Sea's Monsters and the World They Live In* (Buffalo, NY: Firefly Books, 2014), p. 99.

4. Jonathan Bird, "Echinoderms: The Spiny Animals," Oceanic Research Group, updated June 5, 2007, http://www.oceanicresearch.org/education/wonders/echinoderm.html.

5. David Braun, "Sea Lilies Evolved Escape Strategy from Predators over 200 Million Years," *National Geographic* blog, March 23, 2010, https://blog.nationalgeographic.org/2010/03/23/sea-lilies-evolved-escape-strategy-from-predators-over-200-million-years/.

6. "Sea Cucumber Poop Is Surprisingly Good for the Ecosystem," *National Geographic*, April 29, 2018, https://video.nationalgeographic.com/video/news/00000165-864a-d17a-a967-fecb073a0000.

7. Hoyt, p. 100.

Glossary

abyss An extremely deep area.

bioluminescent Describes living organisms that make their own light, for example, fireflies.

cephalopod An animal, such as an octopus or squid, that has its limbs attached to its head.

chemosynthesis The process of using chemicals instead of light to produce food.

enzyme A protein that causes chemical reactions in plants and animals.

hydrothermal vent A crack in the seafloor that allows super-heated water and minerals to flow into and out of Earth's crust.

mantle The large muscle behind an octopus's or squid's head that holds all of its organs.

marine biologist A scientist who studies life in the oceans.

oceanography The study of the ocean.

pelagic zone An area used to classify characteristics of the ocean, which includes *epipelagic, mesopelagic, bathypelagic, abyssopelagic*, and *hadopelagic*.

ROV A remotely operated vehicle used to explore the ocean.

symbiotic relationship The interaction of different organisms
that enables both to survive.

tectonic plate A large, slow-moving section of Earth's crust.

working theory An idea of how something works, which
develops and changes as new data arises.

Further Reading

Books

Hestermann, Josh, and Bethanie Hestermann. *Marine Science for Kids: Exploring and Protecting Our Watery World*. Chicago, IL: Chicago Review Press, 2017.

Rosenstock, Barb. *Otis and Will Discover the Deep: The Record-Setting Dive of the Bathysphere*. New York, NY: Little, Brown and Company, 2018.

Swanson, Jennifer. *Astronaut-Aquanaut: How Space Science and Sea Science Interact*. Washington, DC: National Geographic Kids, 2018.

Websites

Deep Sea Challenge
www.deepseachallenge.com
Join explorer and filmmaker James Cameron on his record-tying dive into the Mariana Trench.

National Geographic: Oceans
www.nationalgeographic.com/environment/habitats/ocean
Read more about recent deep-sea creature sightings.

Smithsonian Education: Deep Sea
ocean.si.edu/ecosystems/deep-sea
Learn more about Earth's oceans and the creatures that live there.

Index